Lance Armstrong

By Sandy Donovan

AMAZING
ATHLETES

LERNERSPORTS/**Minneapolis**

This book is available in two editions:
Library binding by LernerSports
Soft cover by First Avenue Editions
Imprints of Lerner Publishing Group
241 First Avenue North
Minneapolis, MN 55401 U.S.A.

Website address: www.lernerbooks.com

Library of Congress Cataloging-in-Publication Data

Donovan, Sandra, 1967–
   Lance Armstrong / by Sandy Donovan.
       p.   cm.—(Amazing athletes)
   Includes index.
   ISBN: 0–8225–3691–9 (lib. bdg. : alk. paper)
   ISBN: 0–8225–2039–7 (pbk. : alk. paper)
   Armstrong, Lance—Juvenile literature. 2. Cyclists—United States—Biography—Juvenile literature.
[1. Armstrong, Lance. 2. Bicyclists. 3. Cancer—Patients.] I. Title. II. Series.
GV1051.A76D66 2005
796.6'2'092—dc22
                                                                              2003023306

Manufactured in the United States of America
1 2 3 4 5 6 –DP–10 09 08 07 06 05

TABLE OF CONTENTS

Lance Armstrong focuses on pedaling during the 2004 Tour de France. Many experts say this bike race is the world's most difficult sports event.

CLIMBING THE MOUNTAIN

What a difference a year made to Lance Armstrong! During the 2003 **Tour de France** bicycle race, he had fought illness most of the time. But at the 2004 Tour, he was in top form—and it showed.

Each July, the world's best **cyclists** gather for the Tour de France. This is bicycle racing's toughest race. It winds for more than 2,000 miles and is made up of parts, called **stages**. Some stages are flat. Others go up steep mountains. Climbing steep mountains is Lance's specialty.

In 2003, though, Lance struggled to keep up. Other riders were challenging him as they never had before. At one point, a fan's bag caught his handlebar, and he fell to the pavement.

In 2003, Lance crashed in the fifteenth stage of the race. He just barely won the 2003 Tour.

But in 2004, he pedaled his bike with ease. He had lots of energy, and he looked relaxed. He won six stages, four of them in the mountains. The major riders had changed too. He took on young German and Italian riders and beat them time after time. In 2003, Lance had barely won his fifth-in-a-row Tour de France. In 2004, he

Lance looked relaxed and happy throughout the 2004 Tour.

simply couldn't be beaten. He won his sixth Tour—the only man in cycling history to do so.

Six in a row is amazing. But for Lance, any win felt amazing. Eight years earlier, he had nearly died from a disease called **cancer**. Every time he won a race, he felt happy to be alive.

The Tour lasts more than three weeks. Riders can spend up to eight hours a day on their bikes. The Tour finishes in Paris, the capital of France.

Lance holds up six fingers—one for each Tour win.

Lance is close to his mom *(left)*, who raised him alone. She worked her way up from low-paid jobs to become a business executive.

THE YOUNG ATHLETE

Lance Armstrong was born September 18, 1971, and grew up in Plano, Texas. His mother, Linda, divorced his father when Lance was a baby. Linda believed that you should never quit, no matter what the odds. She taught Lance to work hard and to never give up.

At Lance's elementary school, most of the boys played football or baseball. Lance wanted to play these sports too. But he wasn't fast enough to be very good. Instead, Lance found he had another talent. He could run for a long time, longer than anyone else. He wasn't the fastest runner, but he didn't get tired as fast as the other kids.

Soon, he started running in long races. He practiced hard and ran six miles every day after school. Lance learned he had **stamina**—the energy and strength to do something for a long time. He also didn't like to lose.

In Texas, Lance's home state, people are crazy about football. Lance felt left out when he found he couldn't play the sport well.

Lance began taking part in triathlons at a young age.

Before long, Lance had added swimming and bicycling to running. All these sports require stamina. They are also the three parts of a difficult sport called the **triathlon.** In a triathlon, athletes swim, *then* cycle, and *then* run, all in the same race. In 1984, at the age of thirteen, Lance won the Iron Kids Triathlon.

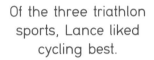

Of the three triathlon sports, Lance liked cycling best.

BECOMING A CYCLIST

Lance was becoming a top athlete. In high school, Lance won two national triathlon championships. He was the best young athlete in the country at his sport. He knew he wanted to become a **professional,** or paid, athlete after he finished school.

Of all sports, Lance loved to race his bicycle. It's true that he loved to win triathlons. But he didn't love running or swimming as much as he loved cycling. So, after high school, he decided to focus on bicycle racing. He moved to Austin, Texas, and spent all his time cycling.

Lance also liked racing as part of a team. Cycling may not seem like a team sport, but it really is. Without the help of their teammates, cyclists would not win races. Teammates ride in front of the team leader and protect the rider from the wind. It takes more energy to pedal in front through the wind. With the help of teammates, the leader can save energy for the end of the

Lance began entering bike races during high school. He competed against riders years older than he was.

The rider at the front of a cycling team blocks the wind. This cyclist helps the team leader save energy for later in the race.

race. Cycle racing also requires hard work and a strong will to win.

In 1990, when he was nineteen, Lance won eleventh **place** at the World Championship Road Race in Utsunomiya, Japan. This was a 115-mile race on a tough course with a long, steep mountain climb. The next year, Lance was also named the U.S. **amateur,** or unpaid, cycling champion.

Most cycling teams have a leader and eight other riders. These riders are called *domestiques*, a French word that means supporter or helper.

Meanwhile, a cycling team called Subaru-Montgomery asked Lance to join it as one of their team leaders. With his new team, Lance won a difficult eleven-day race in Italy. Cyclists all over the world were beginning to know who Lance Armstrong was.

After Lance became famous, people wanted to know more about him. Here, he poses with his Harley motorcycle.

FINDING FAME

In 1992, Lance raced for the United States in the Summer Olympics in Barcelona, Spain. He thought he would win a medal. Instead, he came in fourteenth. Lance was disappointed to do so badly at the Olympics. The next day, he became a professional athlete, or a pro.

In Lance's first race as a pro—the Classico San Sebastian—he fell far behind the other racers. Many cyclists would have quit the race when they were so far behind. But his mother taught him never to be a quitter. Lance pedaled all the way to the finish line. He came in last out of 111 riders.

And he continued to work hard to improve. Lance's hard work began to pay off. He won many races and earned millions of dollars. But that wasn't his real goal. Lance wanted to be road racing's world champion.

In 1993, he got his chance at the World Championship Road Race that was being held in Oslo, Norway. Halfway through the race, Lance hit a wet area on the road and crashed. He got back on his bike, but he thought he had lost too much time to win the race. Then he

Lance celebrated his win at the World Championship Road Race in 1993.

remembered what his mother taught him about quitting. He started pedaling hard. His teammates blocked the wind for him and helped him catch up. A few hours later, he took the lead. He won the race and became the youngest-ever world champion cyclist.

For the next few years, it seemed that Lance could not lose. In 1993 and 1995, he won stages of the Tour de France. In 1995 and 1996,

Lance won back-to-back Tours du Pont in 1995 and 1996.

he won the **Tour du Pont,** the most famous bike race in the United States at that time. He represented the United States at the 1996 Olympic Games in Atlanta, Georgia. A French company named Cofidis gave Lance a **contract** to be part of its international racing team.

The twelve-day Tour du Pont covered about 1,100 miles. Riders raced a course that went through Delaware, Virginia, North Carolina, and South Carolina.

Lance rode in the 1996 Olympic races. He couldn't have known that cancer had already taken over his body.

SETBACK

In the fall of 1996, though, Lance began feeling ill. He thought he had worn himself out racing too hard. He began coughing up blood. This was serious, and he knew he had to see a doctor. He thought the doctor would tell him to take it easy for a while. Instead, the doctor had scary news—Lance had cancer.

Doctors operated in October 1996 to remove the cancer throughout Lance's body. They told him he would probably die in less than a year. To make matters worse, Cofidis ended its contract with Lance.

But Lance had other things on his mind. To fight his cancer, he had to have a treatment called **chemotherapy.** In this treatment, doctors use needles to put a powerful medicine into the body. The medicine kills the cancer, but it makes the person very sick. Lance lost his hair and couldn't walk. He threw up all the time.

The doctors changed Lance's chemotherapy so that his lungs wouldn't be hurt by the strong medicine.

Lance had chemotherapy for three months. He lost all his strength. He thought he would never ride his bike again, even if he lived. But soon, he was gaining strength. In October 1997, he had his one-year checkup. The doctor said Lance had no more cancer. He began bicycle racing again. And another **sponsor**— the United States Postal Service (USPS)— accepted Lance as a member of its pro cycling team.

In 1997, Lance was recovering from cancer instead of racing.

Lance wears the colors of his sponsor, the United States Postal Service (USPS) in the Ride for the Roses. This annual cycling event in Texas raises money for the Lance Armstrong Foundation.

Another great thing happened to Lance when he was getting better from cancer. When he was receiving chemotherapy, he met Kristin Richard. They eventually married.

Lance didn't forget what it was like to be sick. He set up the Lance Armstrong Foundation to help pay for cancer studies and to give hope to cancer victims.

Tour de France Champion

Lance said that beating cancer was the hardest thing he had ever done. He knew that his life would never be the same again. He learned how much he loved life when he almost died.

Lance decided that he would work as hard as he could to get back his strength. He rode his bike around his home in Texas every day. Then he moved to Europe to **train** with his USPS team. He slowly made his way back to the top of the pro cycling

Four jerseys (shirts) are awarded during the Tour. The overall leader wears yellow. The best climber wears polka dots. Green is for the best sprinter. And white is for the best rookie rider.

In 1999, Lance celebrated his first Tour de France win.

world. His new goal was to prepare to race in the 1999 Tour de France with USPS. Nobody in racing expected Lance and his team to win. After all, he had been dying from cancer only two years earlier.

But Lance did win, not only for himself but for cancer victims around the world. His life changed even further that year when Kristin gave birth to their son, Luke.

In 2002, Lance won his fourth Tour de France. He stands on the podium with his family. (He and his wife later split up.)

The next year, Lance surprised everyone again. He won the Tour de France for the second time in a row, proving that his 1999 win wasn't just luck. Then he won again in 2001. He again followed up a Tour win with a new family addition. Kristin gave birth to twin girls, Isabelle and Grace, later that year.

In 2002, Lance became the first American to win the Tour de France four times in a row. In

2003, he became only the fifth person in history to win the Tour five times.

None of the men who had won five Tours had won a sixth. As the 2004 Tour started in July, Lance and his USPS team were in great form.

By winning the 2003 Tour, Lance joined four other men who had also won five Tours. Three of them—*(from left)* Bernard Hinault, Eddie Merckx, and Miguel Induráin—posed with Lance.

The team worked together to keep Lance among the race leaders. In the mountains, Lance took the lead and never looked back. He became the only man to win six Tours, all of them in a row!

Lance also got a new sponsor. USPS gave way to the Discovery Channel. Lance is set up to keep making history—both as a cyclist and as a cancer survivor.

Lance enters Paris surrounded by his USPS teammates to win his sixth Tour.

Selected Career Highlights

2004 Won a record sixth Tour de France, the only person to do so
Won second ESPY as Best Male Athlete

2003 Won his fifth Tour de France
Won ESPY as Best Male Athlete

2002 Won his fourth Tour de France
Named Sportsman of the Year by *Sports Illustrated*
Named Male Athlete of the Year by the Associated Press

2001 Won his third Tour de France

2000 Won his second Tour de France
Won a bronze medal at the Olympic Games in Sydney, Australia

1999 Won his first Tour de France

1998 Placed fourteenth in his first race since becoming sick from cancer
Won four other cycling races

1997 Returned to cycling after fighting cancer
Signed with USPS cycling team

1996 Won his second Tour du Pont
Placed twelfth at the Olympic Games in Atlanta, Georgia
Was told he had cancer

1995 Won his first Tour du Pont

1994 Placed second at the Tour du Pont

1993 Finished first in all three races of the Thrift Drug Triple Crown
Won the U.S. National Road Race Championship
Won the World Championship Road Race in Norway
Placed second at the Tour du Pont
Won a stage of the Tour de France for the first time

1992 Placed fourteenth at the Olympic Games in Barcelona, Spain

1991 Won the Settimana Bergamasca, an eleven-day race in Italy
Named U.S. National Amateur Champion in cycling

1990	Won national Sprint-Course Triathlon championship again
	Placed eleventh at World Championship Road Race in Japan
	Earned second place at U.S. National Team Time Trial Championship
1989	Won national Sprint-Course Triathlon championship
1988	Named Rookie of the Year by *Triathlete* magazine
1984	Won Iron Kids Triathlon

Glossary

amateur: someone who receives no prize money for playing in a sporting event

cancer: a serious disease in which some cells in the body grow fast and destroy healthy cells and organs

chemotherapy: the use of chemicals to kill cancer cells

contract: a written deal signed by a cyclist and his or her team

cyclist: a person who participates in the sport of bicycle racing

place: where a cyclist ranks, compared to other cyclists in a race. The winner of a race takes first place.

professional: someone who is paid for playing a sport

sponsor: a company that pays an athlete in support of an activity

stage: a part of a long bicycle race. The Tour de France has twenty stages.

stamina: the energy and strength to keep doing a physically tiring activity for a long time

Tour de France: a famous bicycle race that takes place each July in France

Tour du Pont: a famous bicycle race that took place until 1996 in the eastern United States

train: to prepare oneself by practicing. Athletes train for competitions.

triathlon: a sport in which athletes run, swim, and bicycle, all in the same race

Further Reading & Websites

Armentrout, David, and Patricia Armentrout. *Lance Armstrong*. New York: The Rourke Book Co., 2003.

Armstrong, Kristin. *Lance Armstrong: The Race of His Life*. New York: Grosset & Dunlap, 2000.

Berry, S. L., and Skip Berry. *Tour de France*. Mankato, MN: The Creative Company, 1997.

Garcia, Kimberly. *Lance Armstrong*. New York: Mitchell Lane Publishers, 2002.

Jones, Brenn. *Learning about Resilience from the Life of Lance Armstrong*. New York: PowerKids Press, 2002.

Saviola, Joseph A. *The Tour De France: Solving Addition Problems Involving Renaming*. New York: PowerKids Press, 2004.

Stewart, Mark. *Sweet Victory: Lance Armstrong*. Brookfield, CT: Millbrook Press, 2000.

The Junior Cycling Athlete: Getting Started
<http://www.members.aol.com/JrCycAthl/getstart/Getstart.html>
This website has all the information you need to get started as a cyclist. Find out about the equipment you need, how to find races, and training tips.

Lance's Official Website
<http://www.lancearmstrong.com>
Visit Lance Armstrong's official website to find more information about the cyclist. The site includes a photo gallery, stories about the champion, and a schedule of his upcoming races and events.

Sports Illustrated for Kids
<http://www.sikids.com>
Find out more about the sport of cycling as well as about other famous cyclists.

Index

Photo Acknowledgments

Photographs are used with the permission of: © Doug Pensinger/Getty Images, p. 4; © Reuters NewMedia, Inc./CORBIS, pp. 5, 25; © Joel Saget/AFP/ Getty Images, pp. 6, 28; © AFP/Getty Images, pp. 7, 17; © AP/Wide World Photos, pp. 8, 22; © Stephen Dunn/Getty Images, pp. 10, 11; © Paolo Cocco/ AFP/Getty Images, p. 13; © Mike Powell/Getty Images, pp. 15, 18; © Pascal Rondeau/Getty Images, p. 20; © Jay G. Carraway/Getty Images, p. 23; © Stefano Rellandini/Reuters/CORBIS, p. 26; © Reuters/CORBIS, p. 27; © Tim de Waele/CORBIS, p. 29.

Cover: © Icon SMI.